Katie DaCosta

GOA, FOOD, AND ME

Traditional and unique Goan recipes made modern and personal

Goa, Food, and Me

Author: Katie DaCosta

Copyright © Katie DaCosta (2023)

The right of Katie DaCosta to be identified as author of this work has been asserted by the author in accordance with section 77 and 78 of the Copyright, Designs and Patents Act 1988.

First Published in 2023

ISBN: 978-1-915996-28-2 (Hardback)
978-1-915996-29-9 (eBook)

Book cover design and layout by:

White Magic Studios
www.whitemagicstudios.co.uk

Published by:

Maple Publishers
Fairbourne Drive, Atterbury,
Milton Keynes,
MK10 9RG, UK
www.maplepublishers.com

A CIP catalogue record for this title is available from the British Library.

All rights reserved. No part of this book may be reproduced or translated by any form or by any means, electronic or mechanical, including photocopying, recording or by any information storage and retrieval system without written permission from the author.

Katie DaCosta

About

Katie DaCosta writes from the heart and has written this Goan Cookbook which blends Goan recipes and culture while giving you a unique window into the region and the REAL GOA. She will take you on her own journey of sights, tastes, and cultural experiences with a personal touch.

Full of mouth-watering recipes, some traditional, some with a unique twist and new ones with a hint of Goa.

With the growth of Vegetarianism and Veganism, she offers alternatives to fish and meat in some of the dishes.

Today, as an International business and Inclusion leader, she recognises the power of diversity of cuisine in bringing and uniting people of different cultures together.

She wants to bring the REAL, delicious and hidden GOA to everyone through these much-loved personal recipes, fond memories and cultural insights.

Preface

Welcome to My Goa!

Welcome to My Cookbook: Goa, Food and Me

I'm bringing you my personal collection of Goan recipes with a twist, mixing it up with some of my Goan heritage made personal and some originally created spicy recipes. I've even added some tourism insights on Goa taken from my many visits. You'll see these scattered throughout the book.

Goa has a unique cuisine and culture where East meets West. That's why so many tourists today flock to its golden beaches, beautiful nature, culture, exotic food and friendly laid-back lifestyle.

If you know a real Goan well, you will know we love food, drink, and, most of all, enjoying it with friends and family with lots of music and dancing thrown in.

There is always an open house somewhere, and we welcome everyone. We are truly inclusive.

I've created this Cookbook with a personal touch and fond recollection of the delicious dishes I grew up with, which my mother passed on to me, and now I can pass them on to you!

I have to also thank my late father as he was the chief food taster of every single dish providing useful inputs and changes to the ingredients making them what they are today.

Knowing the importance of the growth of Vegetarianism and Veganism today, many of the recipes with meat and fish can be substituted with tofu, paneer, egg, or more meatier vegetables.

Goan cuisine is so versatile down to the unique mix of spices and ingredients.

As a Diversity and Inclusion leader, I truly believe food brings all cultures and people together. It's the one thing that unites us in the name of inclusion, no matter who we are!

I hope you enjoy this Cookbook as much as I have enjoyed creating it for you!

With love,

Katie xx

A little about Goa to start off with!

Even though colonisation is never easy for those being ruled, Goa would not be what it is today if it was not for the Portuguese influence. It was only in 1961, after a 450-year rule when Goa was integrated back into India. Portuguese as a language was also widely spoken during colonisation, and some of the older generation of Goans, going back to my grandparents are still fluent in it. It's not surprising to realise that many Goans will have Portuguese heritage and blood within them from this long rule, my father being one of them.

The Portuguese certainly left their legacy. Visit Goa now, and you will still see the remnants of this with a Catholic population with their own language, the Indo-European Konkani, albeit it is now in the minority due to the influx of other Indians.

True Goans will have Portuguese surnames like DaSilva, DeSouza, Fernandez, Dias, DaCunha, and there are many more.

The Portuguese influence is also very visible. Beautiful churches are everywhere.

Don't miss a visit to Olde Goa to visit the stunning Basilica of Bom Jesus, where the body of St Francis Xavier is housed.

Goa is a gem where a coastal location, and a unique culture can be found, which made it such an attractive place to conquer and now to visit.

Tourism is big business here. And why wouldn't it be, with golden stretches of sandy beaches, affordable and delicious food and drinks, beachside hotels, nightlife, jungles, waterfalls, and spice plantations, all the way up to the hippie markets in the North.

So, now, let's get to the food because that's why you are reading this, right?

Goan cuisine is unlike any other Indian food. It is the perfect blend of coastal living, with fish, shellfish, coconut, and vinegar playing a huge part in the cuisine.

For those who are brave enough, do try the local liquor Cashew Feni or Coconut Feni, which are only sold in Goa.

I guarantee you won't have tasted anything like it before.

Goa and Me

I was under two years old when I arrived in England to join my parents, to make a better life for themselves, but Goa has never left me.

I've been to Goa a smattering of times in my lifetime, but every time that plane touches down on the sacred ground, I sigh in relief as if I have come home. It's funny, as I have had a completely British upbringing in every way, but the love of the place is still very much there.

My parents arrived in the seventies when racism was rife. It was not easy for them to find somewhere to live with doors being shut in their face. My late father had served in the Royal Navy, and having travelled the world, it was now time to settle down roots, and he decided to make England his home, as well as ours. My father was certainly a handsome and stylish man especially down to his mixed Portuguese-Goan background, and a lot of the recipe tastes and ingredients have been inspired by his childhood. He was obviously our Chief food taster. He actually inspired my mother to come up with many of the recipes today and enjoyed experimenting and passing on tips from his father who was a great cook himself.

My parents certainly did face trials coming to the UK, as did so many other Goans.

But despite the trials they faced, I am super proud of the life they made here, especially integrating into the British way of life and sharing the Goan culture through food and drink.

It certainly helps that Goans like to socialise. Good food and drink always go hand in hand. My family home most weekends became a place for social gatherings. My mother would be busy making Goan snacks, curries, rice, and salads at the last minute. She was so quick and nimble; she could make anything taste amazing and always made a feast from absolute scratch. No frozen food or ready-prepared food anywhere.

My father of course, would be busy making sure he had enough alcohol and music sounds for an all-night party. As a child, the house was always buzzing at weekends. We would always have a Goan friend or two dropping in unannounced for a chat and a drink, but I do miss the buzz even today.

So, no wonder Goa is regarded as a party place where beach parties and delicious, fresh beachside meals come together. Don't forget to wash that down with the abundance of cocktails, a lime-soda or a cold refreshing beer.

There are restaurants in abundance, but I prefer to eat beachside at a beach shack any day or night. The food is tasty and very affordable with a picture postcard view of golden sand, the sea and shack music. Heaven.

Goan Kitchen Basics

Want to cook like a real Goan?

Make sure you stock up on the essentials. They are all easily available in supermarkets and Asian food stores.

In every real Goan kitchen, you will find spice essentials. Many of these can be bought in powder form, but if you want a more authentic taste, which is preferable, you can grind these yourself, which is what most Goans do. Most Goan kitchens will have a spice grinder to make fresh spice powders. I find coffee grinders work really well and are very affordable.

Common spices and powders you will find are turmeric, cardamoms, cinnamon, black pepper, garam masala, cumin, chilli, cloves, and coriander powder.

Add an abundance of coriander leaves, onion and lots of garlic and ginger.

And with our love for coastal living, coconut is widely used. In Goa, fresh coconut is grated for cooking, but desiccated coconut works just as well.

If you are feeling adventurous, you can purchase a coconut grinder.

Let's not forget the importance that shellfish and fish play in the cuisine, with Mackerel, Kingfish, Pomfret, Clams, Mussels and Prawns being the most popular.

Coconut vinegar is used in many traditional Goan dishes. Normal malt vinegar will work just as well, as it will give the sourness that makes the dishes so unique.

Semolina is also a staple kitchen cupboard item. It is traditionally used rather than breadcrumbs as a coating for croquettes and similar snacks.

It will also feature in Goan desserts.

Important things to note before we get cooking

Measurements

Teaspoon is abbreviated tsp.

Tablespoon is abbreviated tbsp.

Measurements are in grams & milliliters.

When cooking rice, we use a cup that is equivalent to a coffee cup sized.

1 cup of rice will need the equivalent of 1.5 cups of water when cooking.

Cooking methods

We will use a combination of cooking techniques which includes frying, baking, steaming, blanching, boiling, and grilling.

When shallow frying:

The oil will come at least halfway up to whatever you are frying.

When deep frying:

The oil will completely cover whatever you are frying, and it will be submerged.

How to skin a tomato:

Place the tomatoes in a bowl of boiling water for at least a minute. This will make the skins easier to peel off and ready for cooking.

Home-made breadcrumbs:

I find homemade breadcrumbs taste so much more intense in flavour.

- Place stale or unwanted bread in a hot oven for at least 5 minutes. Turn the heat off and leave it to cool.
- If the bread is not crispy enough, just oven it for a few more minutes.
- Break the bread up into small pieces.
- Blitz in a blender until the bread resembles fine breadcrumbs.
- Store in a sealed container and use it when you need it.

Spices

For a truly authentic Goan taste, I would recommend dry-roasting whole spices in a hot pan before grinding. This will only take a few minutes, and ensure you stir throughout to prevent burning. There is nothing worse than the taste of burnt spices.

However, I realise it's a lot easier to use ready-made spice powders, which are easily available.

Feel free to use whatever is more convenient for you.

Note: If the recipe states 1 tsp. of cumin seeds, just use the equivalent of 1 tsp. of cumin powder.

Let's get going!

My Personal Recipes

Popular Goan Beverages
The Famous Everyday Lime Soda 2

Appetisers and snacks
Golden Goan Egg Roll 6
Papad Parcels 8
Crispy Aubergine Slices 10
Roadside Goan Croquettes 12
Rava Masala Prawns 14
Fishcakes 16
Tourism insight: Market life 20

Goans need a Side dish too
Potato & Onion Masala 24
Goan Green Chutney 26
Steamed Coconut Sana 28
Spicy Spinach Side 30
Coconut Courgettes 31
Goan Puri 32
Yoghurt Roti 34
Tourism insight: Beach life 38

All the mains
King Prawn Pilau 42
Yellow Pilau 44
Creamy Caldin Curry 46
Grandad's Roast Green pork 48
Green Chicken Cafreal 50
Lamb Xacuti 52
Chickpea Xacuti 54
Spicy Goan Noodles 56
Spicy Goan meatballs 58
Chicken Tikka masala 60
Sorpotel 62
Goan Fish Curry 64
Okra and Prawn Curry 66
Goan Chilly Fry 68
Stuffed Spice peppers 70
Chilli-Cheese Omelette 72
Green Goan Garlic Chicken 74
Tourism insight: Church life 78

Sweet stuff
Bolinha Semolina Cookies 80
Goan Nevri Pastries 82
Kormolas Anytime Crunch 84
Rainbow Layered Bebinca 86
Vermicelli angel hair dessert 88
Coconut & Jaggery Pancakes 90
Tourism insight: Spice trail 93

A bit about Goan Pickles 94

Beverages in Goa

A quick dive into the traditional Goan drinks including Feni with a recipe for Lime-Soda, which is a personal favourite.

A Feni a day keeps the sadness at bay!

Tip back a Cashew or Coconut Feni. I dare you.

You won't be able to buy this alcoholic drink anywhere outside of Goa. However, if you are lucky enough to make friends with a Goan, they may just allow you to try it.

Made from the Cashew nut's fruit or the Coconut palm, it's the tequila of Goa.

Just drink it straight, or try it heated with a little sugar, purely for medicinal purposes for a sore throat and coughs. I Promise!

Traditionally it is used in Goan cooking. Coconut Feni is normally used in the Goan steamed "Sana." You'll find a recipe for it right here in this book.

Port Wine is also available in Goa. You'll find it on the menu. It is affordable, sweet, and very easy to drink and was another gastronomic introduction from the Portuguese.

When in Goa, don't forget to stop roadside and try sugarcane

Juice straight from the cane.

It's surprisingly not that sweet, very refreshing and with a burst of lime juice, so very delicious and thirst quenching in the heat.

The Famous Everyday Lime Soda
Sweet or Salt, Ma'am?

PREPARATION TIME
5 MINS

SERVINGS
1

A trip to Goa is incomplete if you have not had the refreshing but very simple Lime soda.

Have it sweet or salty, or a bit of both. So simple to make, but I only seem to crave it when in Goa. It must be something to do with the locals, sun, and extra fresh limes!

Lime soda is basically fresh citrus juice and soda water with a little added sugar and some salt based on your personal preference.

Ingredients

The juice of 1 fresh lime according to taste

0.5 tsp. Salt

0.5 tsp. Sugar

250ml Extra cold soda water or sparkling water

Slice of lime to serve

Add more salt or sugar for personal taste

Method

Add fresh lime juice to a glass.

Add the salt and sugar and mix well.

Add the cold soda water. Stir well.

Add a garnish of fresh lime and serve.

So simple, and if there is a beach nearby, relax and watch the world go by, or you can always pretend.

Tip 😊

Add a dash of Gin or Vodka for an interesting twist

Appetisers & Snacks

*Goans can't have a drink without
a snack or two.*

Goan pastries made in heaven

A trip to Goa would not be complete without trying some of its mouth-watering snacks. Goans always need a snack or two to accompany a drink, whether it be tea, soda, beer, or something stronger.

When in Goa, I pull up and buy spiced meat patties, fish patties, and croquettes roadside for takeaway. You can also visit one of the many bakeries or cafes in Goa for a larger selection.

My favourite café is Xaviers in Mapsua which is well known and has been around for 90 years, I've been told.

It was my father's favourite, which he used to visit as a child, which then became my favourite. I am sure it was my grandpa Dominic's favourite as well.

It's my regular stop-off whenever in North Goa. It's always busy, with extra friendly staff who always stop for a chat, and let's not forget the delicious flaky pastries, but the prawn rissoles always seem to sell out before I get there.

Wash them down with a cold soda or a Kingfisher beer and enjoy the ambiance and friendly chat with the locals and passing tourists.

So, my Cookbook would not be complete without a few Goan snack recipes you will want to make again and again.

Golden Goan Egg Rolls

 **PREPARATION TIME** 20 MINS

 COOKING TIME 10 MINS

 **SERVINGS** 12

Goans are so versatile and can make deliciousness with the most basic ingredients. Whilst fish and meat are featured often in Goan cuisine, here's a twist to cater to our vegetarian friends. The Goan egg roll is a strong competitor to the British Scotch egg, only tastier, in my opinion!

Ingredients

6 Medium potatoes

2 Medium finely chopped onions

1 tsp. Ginger & garlic paste

50g or Half a small bunch of chopped coriander leaves

0.5 tsp. Salt

6 Hard-boiled eggs (peeled)

2 tbsp. Vegetable oil

1 Beaten egg (to dip rolls in)

Enough semolina to cover the egg rolls

Enough vegetable oil to shallow fry the egg rolls

Spices

1 tsp. Garam masala powder

0.25 tsp. Turmeric powder

0.5 tsp. Chilli flakes

Method

Peel, wash, and boil potatoes until soft.

When boiled, mash the potatoes well.

Fry the onions in 1 tbsp. of oil until crispy.

Take off the heat, and add the ginger and garlic paste.

Add the salt and spices.

Add the mashed potato & mix together.

Cut the boiled eggs in half.

Add a little oil to the palms of your hands.

Take a ball size of the potato mixture, and flatten into a disc.

Add an egg half on top and fold the potato mixture around the egg until it is covered.

Dip into beaten egg.

Roll into semolina until fully covered.

Shallow fry in a large deep fry pan on a medium heat until golden brown.

Drain off any oil on a kitchen towel & serve.

Tip 😊

Serve as an appetiser or a tea-time snack. You can even try replacing the egg with prawns, but then it wouldn't be an egg roll, but it will taste just as delicious.

Papad Parcels

PREPARATION TIME
10 MINS

COOKING TIME
15 MINS

SERVINGS
10

I have found this is a great way to jazz up the humble Poppadum the Goan way.

Ingredients

250g Fresh prawns (deveined)

10 Poppadum's

2 Medium chopped onions

15g Chopped ginger

4 Cloves chopped garlic

0.25 tsp. Salt

1 tbsp. Goan Recheado masala. (if you cannot get Recheado masala, use Red Chilli paste instead)

100g Chopped coriander leaves (small bunch)

1-2 tbsp. Vegetable oil (to fry onions, ginger & garlic)

Enough Vegetable oil to deep fry the Poppadum's

Method

Fry the onions, ginger & garlic in oil on a medium heat in a pan until golden.

Cut the prawns into small pieces and add to the pan. Stir and cook until pink.

Add a tablespoon of Goan Recheado Masala or Red Chilli paste.

Cook together, stirring well for 5 minutes.

Add the chopped coriander leaves.

Add salt and mix well.

Turn off the heat, and let the mixture cool down.

Soak the Poppadum's one by one in lukewarm water for about 15 seconds until slightly soft. Drain well on a kitchen towel until dry.

Take the drained Poppadum's and add enough prawn mixture into the centre of the Poppadum.

Fold the Poppadum in a parcel shape. They should be soft and malleable.

Deep fry in hot oil until the Poppadum is cooked and crispy.

I recommend eating these immediately, as they will become soggy if kept for too long.

Tip 😊

You can fill these parcels with anything.

Try filling them with my Roast green pork or even Goan Noodles.

Crispy Aubergine Slices

PREPARATION TIME
5 MINS

COOKING TIME
10 MINS

Serving is based on the size of the aubergine and your ability to resist eating them one after the other.

I bet you have never had aubergines this way. Such a simple snack that I grew up with. Very dangerous as it's easy to eat the whole stack, which I have done many times. Using an egg masala coating like this gives vegetables extra taste and crisp.

Ingredients

1 Medium sized aubergine

2 Eggs - beaten

2 tsp. Garam masala

1 tsp. Ground pepper

0.5 tsp. Salt

Enough Vegetable oil (to shallow fry the aubergines)

Method

Slice the aubergines into thin slices round ways.

Mix garam masala, pepper, salt, and the beaten eggs in a shallow dish.

Dip the aubergine slices into the egg mix until fully coated.

Ensure the oil is hot in a large shallow pan for frying.

Fry the aubergine slices on both sides until the egg has gone crispy.

Take out and drain on a paper towel.

Eat straight away; otherwise, the aubergines will go soggy.

However, these could be re-crisped in an air-fryer for a later time.

Tip 😊

I've tried this simple recipe with Courgettes, and they taste just as good.

Roadside Goan Croquettes

PREPARATION TIME
30 MINS

COOKING TIME
15 MINS

SERVINGS
20

These spicy meat croquettes are so versatile and tasty. I stop off and grab them roadside when on holiday in Goa.

Ingredients

500g of Minced beef, lamb, or chicken

2 Large chopped onions

25g Finely chopped ginger

10 Finely chopped garlic cloves

2 Finely chopped green chillies

4 Skinned and finely chopped medium tomatoes

1 Diced medium potato

1 tbsp. Vinegar

1 Beaten egg

Semolina (enough to cover the croquettes)

Approx. 150g home-made fine breadcrumbs

100g (small bunch) Chopped coriander leaves

2 tbsp. Oil (to fry onions, ginger, and garlic)

Enough Oil to deep fry the croquettes

Spice mix

0.5 tsp. Cumin powder

0.5 tsp. Black pepper

0.5 tsp. Clove powder

0.5 tsp. Cinnamon powder

1 tsp. Garam masala

1 tsp. Chilli powder

0.5 tsp. Turmeric powder

0.5 tsp. Coriander powder

0.5 tsp. Salt

Method

Heat the oil on a medium heat in a deep fry pan.

Fry the onion, ginger, and garlic until cooked.

Add the chopped tomatoes and fry together until the mixture softens.

Add the minced meat and diced potatoes to the pan.

Cook for another 5 minutes on a high heat until the meat has turned brown.

Turn the heat down and add the vinegar to the pan and stir.

Add all the spice mix to the pan and mix well.

Add the chopped coriander.

Turn the heat up high and cook until the meat fluid has dried.

Take off the heat and allow it to cool.

When cooled, blitz the mixture in a blender until smooth.

Add the beaten egg and home-made breadcrumbs and mix well.

Store the mixture in the fridge for at least 30 minutes to set.

After 30 minutes, take the mixture from the fridge and roll it into small sausage-shaped croquettes.

Roll each croquette in semolina until fully covered.

Deep fry in hot oil until golden brown.

Drain on a paper towel before serving.

Rava Masala Prawns

PREPARATION TIME
25 MINS

COOKING TIME
10 MINS

5 PRAWNS
PER SERVING

This is one of my favourites as I stop for a beach shack snack. When my children were younger, on holiday in Goa, this was all they ate in a day. They even ate the crispy tail. I tried to throw in a salad, but they went for chips instead. A nice twist to our Friday Fish and Chips.

Ingredients

10 Fresh deveined king prawns (with tail)

1 tbsp. Goan Recheado masala. If you cannot get this masala, you can substitute it with Red Chilli paste.

0.5 tsp. Salt

1 tsp. Turmeric powder

1 Beaten egg

Enough Semolina to cover the prawns

Enough Vegetable oil for deep frying the prawns

Method

Add salt, turmeric powder, and the Goan Recheado masala to the prawns.

Mix well and allow to marinate for about 15 minutes.

After 15 minutes, coat the marinated prawns with the beaten egg.

Roll each one in semolina.

Deep fry in hot oil until golden.

Drain on a paper towel and serve.

Tip 😊

You can use this recipe for other shellfish like mussels or oysters.

Serve with mayonnaise or a tomato dip.

It's simply delicious and so easy.

My Favourite Fish Cakes

PREPARATION TIME
20 MINS

COOKING TIME
15 MINS

MAKES
APPROX. 12

This is my personal family recipe which has been handed down from my mother. In fact, it's now become the picnic favourite for all the family as it tastes just as great hot or cold.

Ingredients

2 x 110g Cans of drained tuna

1 Large chopped onion

2 Medium boiled potatoes ready to mash

Approx. 100g Chopped coriander (small bunch)

2 tsp. Garam masala

1 tbsp. Ground pepper

0.5 tsp. Salt

2 Beaten eggs

Enough Golden breadcrumbs to coat the fishcakes

Enough Vegetable oil for shallow frying

Method

Mash the boiled potato, and add the chopped onions, coriander, garam masala, pepper, and salt. Mix well.

Add the drained tuna and continue to mix until evenly distributed.

Form the mixture into flattened balls. Size depends on your preference.

Roll each ball in the beaten egg and fully coat it in breadcrumbs.

Heat oil in a deep fry pan and maintain on a medium heat. You will need enough to shallow fry the fish cakes.

Fry the fishcakes until golden, turning them over to ensure both sides are cooked.

Drain on a paper towel and serve.

Tip 😊

This is a perfect lunch meal with a crunchy Fresh salad and some rice. Can be eaten hot or cold. Try substituting with tinned mackerel or sardines and you can add some green chillies for extra heat if that's what you like.

Notes

Use this page to add any adjustments you may want to make to the recipes based on your personal preference and tastes.

Notes

Market Life

A trip to Goa would not be complete without a visit to a market. The variety of markets is exciting, exhilarating, and blows your senses.

You can buy almost anything here from clothes, food, spices, jewellery, pottery, flowers, materials, tattoos, leathers, tea, food, the list goes on.

Main municipal markets where you will mingle with the locals are so worthy of a trip to see the variety of goods and to experience the ambiance.

I would recommend a visit to Panaji, Margao, or Mapusa for this experience. Margao market is a covered market with a series of indoor mazes with various stalls selling everything from underwear and shoes to teas and spices.

However, the most famous tourist market is the Anjuna flea market in North Goa. Get there early, as it gets busy and the afternoon sun can be very hot in high tourist season.

You can of course stop off in the sidebars for drinks and snacks.

You can even get a fake tattoo or get your hair braided whilst you cool down.

You may also want to look up the night markets available in North Goa if you're going to stay out of the hot sun and have a different experience in the evening.

I don't worry about bringing too many clothes to Goa. There is so much choice at the markets, and I always grab some great summer dresses, beach wear, hats, and sandals at a fraction of the price here. I have even seen some of the dress styles in the market being sold at much higher

prices in European online clothes retailers, so you are really grabbing a fashionable bargain.

Be ready to barter. It can be so much fun, and don't be surprised when you hear the stall owners speaking in British cockney slang just to get a sale and a laugh!

If you visit a municipal market, you will see chains of the tasty Goan sausage Choris hanging. If you don't see this straight away, just follow your nose.

Choris is a famous delicacy in Goa and is a fusion of Portuguese and Indian ingredients.

It is traditionally eaten in a spicy dish with fried onions and sometimes potatoes.

Try it with a Goan Pao bread roll or even as a substitute for the traditional sausage for breakfast.

Choris smells and tastes very similar to the Spanish Chorizo, but a little spicier. They are however made with chunks of pork and spices combined into a sausage.

Going to Goa is always an opportunity to get your five a day in. With so many delicious and exotic fruits on sale in the markets, it's very easy.

Try some local fruits like Papaya, Dragon fruit, Custard fruit and Chikoo which is my favourite. Or you can enjoy the many tropical fruit juices instead.

Side Dishes

*When it Comes to a Meal,
Goans Need to have a Side or Two.*

Potato & Onion Masala

 **PREPARATION TIME** 15 MINS

 **COOKING TIME** 20 MINS

 **SERVINGS** 4-6

This dish is a perfect accompaniment to a meal. I find it always tastes better the day after when the spices have really infused.

Ingredients

6 Medium-sized potatoes

2 Large chopped onions

30g Finely chopped ginger

20g chopped garlic

4 Big tomatoes

1 tsp. Mustard seeds

100g Chopped coriander (small bunch)

4 tbsp. Vegetable oil

2 Large green chillies

5 tbsp. Passata

Spice mix

1 tsp. Turmeric powder

0.5 tsp. Chilli powder

1 tsp. Coriander powder

0.5 tsp. Cumin powder

1 tsp. Garam masala

1 tsp. Salt

Method

Boil the potatoes until cooked but ensure they are not too mushy, as you will be cutting them into chunks.

When cooked, cut potatoes into small 1-inch chunks. Leave to one side.

Blanch the tomatoes in hot water for a few minutes to help remove the skin. Peel the skin off. Cut tomatoes into small pieces.

Heat the oil in a pan on a medium heat. Add mustard seeds and cook for approx. 1 minute. Stir and do not burn.

Add the onion, ginger and garlic. Fry for a few minutes.

Add the chopped tomatoes and cook the mixture until soft.

Add the spice mix, salt, and chillies.

Add the Passata and stir in well.

Turn the heat down and cook for another 5 minutes.

Add the cooked potatoes, mix well, and cook for another 5 minutes.

Add the chopped coriander, stir in, and turn the heat off.

Ready to eat!

Tip 😊
Add to a toasted sandwich with extra spring onion for a spicy change.

Goan Green Chutney

PREPARATION TIME
15 MINS

COOKING TIME
5 MINS

This is the Goan classic sandwich spread which is traditionally eaten with a layer of ham and soft cheese in a tri-colour sandwich. Sandwich time will never be boring again! However, I personally like to use it as a dip, but it's so versatile you choose for yourself.

Ingredients

200g Fresh chopped coriander (large bunch)

1 Small green mango

200g Pack of desiccated coconut (or freshly grated coconut)

2 Large green chillies

10 Garlic cloves

25g Ginger chunks

1 Medium onion

Juice of half a lemon (you may want to add more lemon juice to taste.)

1 tbsp. Sugar

0.5 tsp. Salt

Spice mix

0.5 tsp. Cumin powder

0.25 tsp. Cinnamon powder

0.25 tsp. Black pepper

1 tsp. Oil to fry the onions, garlic and ginger

Method

Peel onion and cut it into big chunks

Roast onion chunks, garlic, and ginger in a hot pan with the oil for about a minute.

Skin and cut the mango into small pieces. Discard the mango stone.

Now place all the ingredients and the spice mix into a blender, and blend into a fine paste.

It may take a few blends, and you may need to add smaller quantities bit by bit, depending on the size of your blender.

Once you have achieved a fine paste, it is ready to spread and stir as you like.

Store in the fridge in a glass container.

Tip 😊

Add this paste as a fresh, zingy chutney to burgers.

Just perfect with a bowl of plain rice or pasta.

It can also make a great base for a curry or pasta sauce.

Steamed Coconut Sana

PREPARATION TIME
4.5 HOURS, INCLUDING FERMENTATION TIME
OVERNIGHT SOAK FOR RICE

COOKING TIME
30 MINS

SERVINGS
10 SMALL SANA DEPENDING ON THE SIZE OF YOUR MOULDS

These traditional coconut bread cakes are unique to Goa. They are traditionally made with Coconut Feni, but we are going to replace with Coconut water instead.

They are eaten as a savoury compliment to a meal, on their own, or with sweet jaggery for a sweetened version.

I like to break a freshly steamed Sana open to release that coco-nutty heaven before I devour it.

Ingredients

400g White rice (Not basmati or long grain. Masoori rice is the best for this dish and is lower in carbs)

200g Desiccated or Freshly grated coconut

600ml (1 pint) Coconut water

2.5 tbsp. Sugar

0.5 tsp. Salt

Approx. 20 grams of yeast.

Make sure you follow the instructions on the packet to make the yeast solution which can then be added to the Sana mixture.

Note: You will need a large steamer or a big pan with a steamer plate that can hold the Sana containers with a lid. You will need separate mini containers or moulds to hold the Sana mixture whilst steaming.

Method

Soak the rice in cold water overnight in a bowl.

Next day, drain any water from the rice.

Blend the rice with the coconut water and grated coconut until it becomes a smooth mixture resembling batter and then place in a large bowl.

Add the sugar, salt and the yeast solution and mix well together.

Cover with tight cling film over the bowl and keep in a warm place for at least 4 hours to develop and rise. (Try an airing cupboard or the warmest room in your house)

When ready, place the mixture in small containers. I like to use round metal bowls bought at an everyday store.

> **Tip** 😊
> Add pieces of jaggery sugar chunks into the mix before steaming for sweet Sana. You can get this at most Asian supermarkets or in the Asian aisle in your supermarket.

Steam the Sana in a steamer or over a large pan of hot water with the lid closed for about 20-30 minutes until firm and bouncy.

Cool, and remove from the containers.

Break open, relish the smell, and eat.

Creamy Spiced Spinach

PREPARATION TIME
10 MINS

COOKING TIME
15 MINS

SERVINGS
4

Eating spinach will never be the same again with this spicy vegetable side. Cooking it this way will ensure spinach is never bland again.

Ingredients

500g of Fresh spinach

2 Medium-sized chopped onions

8 Cloves chopped garlic

25g Chopped ginger

2 Medium-sized tomatoes (skinned and chopped).

100g Chopped coriander leaves

2 tbsp. Oil or butter or Ghee (based on preference)

6 tbsp. Water

0.25 tsp. Salt

Spice mix

0.5 tsp. Cumin powder

0.5 tsp. Turmeric powder

0.5 tsp. Coriander powder

1 tsp. Garam masala

0.5 tsp. Chilli powder

0.5 tsp. Salt

Method

Wash and cut the spinach.

Steam the spinach in a saucepan with the water and salt for 2 minutes. Ensure you keep the lid on.

Take it off the heat and cool down. Remove any excess water.

When cooled down, rough blend the spinach with the coriander leaves.

Heat the oil on a medium heat in a pan. Add the onions, ginger & garlic. Stir and cook for a minute.

Add the tomatoes.

Turn the heat down to low and cook for 5 minutes until softened.

Add the spice mix and salt. Mix and cook for another few minutes.

Add the blended spinach mix.

Cook for another few minutes.

Turn it off, and it's ready to serve.

Tip

This goes really well with the coconut of the Caldin curry. To add some bulk as a dish on its own, add fried paneer or fried potatoes to the spinach.

Coconut Courgettes

PREPARATION TIME
5 MINS

COOKING TIME
10 MINS

SERVINGS
4

No more boiled vegetables. I like to liven up my vegetables and bring out their taste, with courgette being one of my favourites.

Ingredients

3 Courgettes

2 Diced onions

4 tbsp. Desiccated coconut

0.5 tsp. Salt

1 tbsp. Sugar

3 tbsp. Butter or oil (for frying, depending on preference)

Method

Slice the courgettes round ways.

Fry the onion in the butter or oil over a medium heat until soft and browned.

Add the salt and sugar.

Add the courgettes, and fry on a medium heat until cooked through but still crunchy. I like a little char on mine as that gives the courgettes added flavour.

Add the desiccated coconut and cook for another minute.

Ensure you do not over-cook the courgettes to ensure you have a tasty crunch, otherwise, you will end up with mushy courgettes.

Tip
Use this recipe to liven up cauliflower, green beans, and even brussels sprouts.

Goan Puri

PREPARATION TIME
10 MINS

COOKING TIME
10 MINS

SERVINGS
10 PURI DEPENDING ON THE SIZE OF YOUR CUTTER

These Puris are simple to make in very little time. They are an alternative to Indian Chapati or Paratha.

Ingredients

To make the dough

400g of Chapati flour

1 tbsp. Sugar

1 tsp. Salt

2 tbsp. Ghee or butter or oil (depending on preference)

150ml Warm water

Enough vegetable oil to deep fry the Puri

Method

Mix all the dough ingredients in a bowl until it becomes a firm dough.

Roll out into a thin sheet. The thinner it is, the crispier the Puri.

Cut into circular shapes using a cutter. Go for a size of 3 or 4 inches in diameter.

Heat enough oil in a pan to deep fry the Puri.

Fry the Puri on a medium heat, turning it over a few times until it is puffed out and golden on both sides.

Drain on a kitchen towel.

Tip 😊

I like to make a hole in my Puri and add a spicy filling or a curry. Try adding my Potato masala recipe.

Yoghurt Roti

PREPARATION TIME
25 MINUTES: INCLUDING STAND-TIME

COOKING TIME
10 MINS

SERVINGS
10 ROTI DEPENDING ON THE SIZE OF YOUR CUTTER

This Roti is made with plain yoghurt to add to the taste and texture. My mother always says this is a healthy version, but I am not totally convinced. But yoghurt is good for you anyway isn't it?

Ingredients

1 cup Plain flour

350g Greek plain yoghurt

0.5 tsp. Salt

1 tsp. Sugar

1 tsp. Baking powder

Enough vegetable oil to deep fry the Roti

Method

Make a firm dough with all the ingredients, apart from the vegetable oil.

Depending on the consistency you end up with, you may need to add more yoghurt or more flour.

Leave to stand for about 15 minutes.

Roll the dough out onto a floured surface and create a thin layer. The thinner, the crispier.

Cut into circular shapes using a cutter. Go for a size of 3 or 4 inches in diameter.

Heat enough oil in a pan to deep fry the Roti.

Fry the Roti on a medium heat, turning it over a few times until it is puffed out and golden on both sides.

Drain on a kitchen towel.

Tip 😊
You can add some finely chopped chives and spring onions to the dough for some extra flavour

Notes

Use this page to add any adjustments you may want to make to the recipes based on your personal preference and tastes.

Notes

Beach Life

Goa is located on the West coast of India and is a separate state. So naturally, you'll find beaches on the coast. But these are not just any beaches but stretches of uninterrupted golden sand fringed by palm trees and kissed by clear waters.

Visit Colva, Majorda, Leela, Varca, Anjuna, Calangute, Candolim and Baga beaches for the tourist trail. These are the more well-known and busier beaches, but you won't have to fight for a sunbed or parasol like you may have to do in the Mediterranean.

Most beaches will have lifeguards and beach patrols situated in clear view.

The busier beaches will offer beach sports like paragliding at very affordable prices.

I really can't believe how far Goa has come along in a few years from the last time I visited it.

If you see dogs on the beach, many belong to the fishermen or the beach shack owners. They are completely harmless, very calm, and accustomed to people and tourists.

When you walk along the beach stretches, you'll see the beautiful boats that belong to the fishermen. They normally fish in the early hours of the morning or later in the afternoon, so you'll have to time yourself if you want to see them in action when they pull back with their nets and catch.

If you are lucky enough to see the fishermen bring their catch in, you may be able to haggle a price for fresh fish there and then.

Christmas and the New year are great times for visiting Goa. It is common to celebrate on the beach with dinner, music, dancing, and fireworks.

This is certainly worth the experience at least once in your lifetime and you'll make some new friends!

Don't be annoyed if you are pestered to buy trinkets from the beach ladies. They are so friendly and will chat with you in multiple languages, with English, Hindi, Konkani, and Russian being the norm. They are a wealth of knowledge if you are new to Goa and are always happy to stop and impart their knowledge and guide you.

You'll be so surprised at the fluency of their English, and they are multi-lingual.

Beachside dining is common in Goa. In fact, I prefer to have dinner in a beach shack with a table at the edge of the sand. I have no doubt my favourite shacks due to the quality of the food, and the friendliness and hospitality of the owners. Just be aware that many of the Beach shacks will not be open in the lower season, and some may just be opening up in October ready for the Tourist season which generally runs from October up until end of April.

I'm going to let you into a little secret. The last time I was in Goa, I found myself a secluded beach.

If you want to get away from it all, Carmona beach in South Goa is your stop, and there is even a shack for a snack and a drink! In fact, there are probably many more hidden quieter beaches to be discovered, but don't tell anyone.

All the mains

A mix of the traditional with a modern twist

King Prawn Pilau

PREPARATION TIME
15 MINS

COOKING TIME
25 MINS

SERVINGS
4-6

A rice dish that is perfect for any occasion jazzing up the humble yellow Pilau rice. A Goan meal will always have a Pilau rice on the menu.

Ingredients

20-25 King prawns (deveined)

1.5 Cups Basmati rice

2.75 Cups of boiling water

(Note: For every cup of rice, you should add 1.5 cups of water. Ensure you use the same sized cup for the rice and water)

15g Chopped ginger

4 Chopped garlic cloves

4 Medium-sized tomatoes

2 Medium-sized chopped onions

2 Vegetable stock cubes

0.5 tsp. Garam masala powder

1 tsp. Turmeric powder

2 Large bay leaves

2 Large green chilies

0.5 tsp Salt

5 tbsp. Vegetable oil

Prawn Spice Mix

0.5 tsp. Garam masala powder

0.5 tsp. Curry powder

1 tsp. Turmeric powder

Dry Spice Mix

1 Star anise

1 Large stick of cinnamon

10 Cardamom pods

12 Cloves

Method

Wash rice in water until it runs clear. This will remove the starch.

Place the prawns in a bowl and add the Prawn spice mix.

Leave to marinate for about 15 minutes.

Blanch the tomatoes in hot boiling water. Peel the skins off and finely chop them.

Heat the oil in a large saucepan on a medium heat.

Add the dry spice mix to the oil and stir for a minute. Do not burn.

Turn the heat down. Add the chopped onion, ginger, garlic, bay leaves, and chillies. Stir well.

Add the chopped tomatoes and cook until soft and caramelised.

Add the vegetable stock cube, turmeric, garam masala and salt.

> **Tip** 😊
>
> Do you love your seafood? If so, try adding mussels, oysters, or a bit of squid, making it the new Goan Paella!

Add the prawns. Mix well.

Add the washed rice and stir.

Add the boiling water and allow to boil.

When boiled, turn down the heat, cover, and simmer with the lid on for approx. 15 minutes.

Yellow Pilau Rice

PREPARATION TIME
10 MINS

COOKING TIME
20 MINS

SERVINGS
4-6

Pilau rice is a delicious alternative to plain boiled rice and is eaten regularly in Goan cuisine. Here's my recipe, which is a basic, but every Goan will have their own variation.

Ingredients

- 1 Cup basmati rice
- 1.5 Cups of boiling water
- 2 Medium-sized tomatoes
- 2 Medium-sized chopped onions
- 1 Vegetable stock cube
- 3 Large sticks of cinnamon
- 12 Cloves
- 1 tsp. Turmeric powder
- 0.25 tsp. Salt
- 2 tbsp. Vegetable oil

Method

Wash rice for a few times until water runs clear. This will remove the starch. Rinse all the water off.

Blanch the tomatoes in hot boiling water. Peel the skins off and finely chop them.

Heat oil in a saucepan on a medium heat.

Add cloves, cinnamon, and onions. Mix well and cook until the onions are soft.

Add the chopped tomatoes and cook until softened.

Add turmeric, salt, and the vegetable stock cube. Stir well.

Now add the rinsed rice and fry for a minute.

Add the boiling water.

Allow to boil.

Lower the heat and simmer with the lid on for approx. 15 minutes.

Tip 😊

I sometimes throw in finely diced carrots, peas and sweetcorn to jazz the pilau rice up, but it tastes delicious just on its own.

Creamy Caldin Curry

PREPARATION TIME
10 MINS

COOKING TIME
20 MINS

SERVINGS
4-6

This sweet, creamy coconut-based curry is a staple in Goa.

Traditionally made in Goa with clams, you can replace them with prawns or even boiled eggs. However, we are going to make this one with cauliflower for our vegan friends.

Ingredients

- 1 x 400ml Can of coconut milk
- 2 tsp. Tamarind paste
- 4 Cloves chopped garlic
- 15g Chopped ginger
- 1 Chopped onion
- 2 Chopped tomatoes
- 1 Vegetable stock cube
- 0.25 tsp. Salt
- 0.5 tsp. Sugar
- 1 Medium cauliflower
- 2 tbsp. Vegetable oil
- Water (optional if you prefer a thinner curry)

Spice mix

- 0.25 tsp. Turmeric
- 0.25 tsp. Cumin powder
- 1 tsp. Dried coriander
- 0.25 tsp. Chilli powder
- 0.25 tsp. Garam masala

Method

Cut cauliflower into pieces and blanch in a bowl of hot water for about 5 minutes. Then, take out, drain the water and pat dry.

Heat oil on a medium heat in a pan. Add the onion, ginger, and garlic, and cook for a minute.

Add the chopped tomatoes.

Cook until the mixture becomes a soft paste.

Add the spice mix, vegetable stock cube, and tamarind.

Stir together well.

Add the coconut milk.

Add the salt, sugar and stir.

Add the blanched cauliflower. Cover and cook on a low heat for 10 minutes.

Tip 😊

Serve with white Steaming rice. Also makes for a very warming spicy chunky soup if you add a little more water.

Grandad's Roast Green Pork

PREPARATION TIME
15 MINUTES & OVERNIGHT MARINATE

COOKING TIME
45 MINS

SERVINGS
4-6

My Grandpa Dominic knew his flavours. This was a recipe handed down from him to his cooks. Even though I am not a huge pork lover, I can't resist the garlicky, succulent meat.

My quick go-to in the fridge!

Ingredients

1 Kilo pork leg meat (skinned and cut into chunks)

1 tsp. Salt

300ml (0.5 pints) Vinegar

Juice of 2 Lemons

2 tbsp. Vegetable oil

1 Bulb Chopped garlic

50g Chopped ginger

20 Curry leaves

Approx. 10 Whole dried chillies

Spice mix

1 tsp. Black pepper

0.5 tsp. Cumin powder

1 tsp. Turmeric powder

1 tsp. Cinnamon powder

1 tsp. Clove powder

1 tsp. Cardamom powder

Method

Salt the pork chunks with 0.5 tsp. of salt and leave aside.

Mix the chopped ginger & garlic with the vinegar, lemon juice, 0.5 tsp. of salt, and all the spice mix.

Pour over meat. Cover and marinate overnight in the fridge.

The next day, take the meat out to prepare for cooking.

Heat the oil on a medium heat in a large pan with a lid big enough to hold the meat.

Add the curry leaves and the dried chillies to the oil.

Add the marinated meat with its spice mix and juices to the pan.

Allow to boil.

When boiled, cover and slow cook on a low heat in the meat juices for at least 30 minutes.

When cooked, you can keep it in the fridge for up to a week and slice as you need to.

Tip 😊

I like to make a meal of this by slicing the pork and frying with onions, mushrooms, and peppers. It also makes for a great sandwich or pitta filling.

Green Chicken Cafreal

PREPARATION TIME
4 HOURS 10 MINUTES, INCLUDING 4-HOUR MARINATING TIME

COOKING TIME
25 MINS

This is another traditional dish from Goa. However, this one is not as well-known or as widely eaten as others. The use of coriander gives it a unique green colour.

Ingredients

8 Skinned chicken thighs or drumsticks

0.5 tsp. Salt

1 tsp. Lemon juice

100g or 1 Small bunch of chopped coriander

25g of Chopped ginger

10 Cloves of chopped garlic

3 Green chopped chillies

Juice of 1 lemon

4 tbsp. Vinegar

1 Onion roughly chopped into large chunks

4 tbsp. Vegetable oil

Spice mix

0.5 tsp. Cumin powder

0.5 tsp. Black pepper

0.5 tsp. Cinnamon powder

0.5 tsp. Clove powder

0.25 tsp. Cardamom powder

Method

Cut slashes in the chicken to enable the spices to infuse.

Add the salt and 0.5 tsp. lemon juice. Mix and keep aside.

Roast the onion, ginger, and garlic in a pan on a hot heat in 0.5 tsp. of oil. Take off heat and allow to cool.

Mix the coriander, chillies, roasted onion, ginger, and garlic together. Add the rest of the lemon juice and vinegar. Blend them to make a fine paste.

Add the spice mix.

Pour over the chicken.

Marinate for at least 4 hours in a fridge before cooking.

After 4 hours, heat oil on a medium heat in a large fry pan.

Transfer the marinated chicken to the pan and fry for at least 15 minutes until it is cooked through.

Tip 😊

As this is a slightly drier dish, try it as an alternative to a chicken and chips meal.

You can add water while cooking to create more of a curry base if you prefer.

Transfer to an oven dish with its marinade and cook in a hot oven for approx. 10-15 minutes.

Take out and serve.

Lamb Xacuti

PREPARATION TIME
20 MINS

COOKING TIME
60 MINS

SERVINGS
4-6

A very famous Goan Curry. Its unique and rich flavour is down to the roasted spices and coconut. This was a regular much loved dish at every weekend social my parents had.

Ingredients

1 kilo Lean Lamb meat cut into small chunks
100g Desiccated coconut
0.5 tsp. Salt
Juice of 2 lemons
0.25 tsp. Turmeric powder
3 Large diced onions
4 Medium-sized chopped tomatoes
50g Chopped fresh ginger
16 Cloves chopped garlic
20 Curry leaves
1 tsp. Sugar
300ml (0.5 pint) Water
3 tbsp. Vegetable oil

Masala mix

Whole 5 dried chillies
1 tsp. Cumin seeds
2 Star anise
0.5 tsp. Black peppercorns
0.5 tsp. Cloves
1-inch long Cinnamon stick
0.5 tsp. Cardamom seeds
1 tsp. Poppy seeds (optional)
1 tsp. Fennel seeds
0.5 tsp. Grated nutmeg
0.5 tsp. Mace
2 tsp. Dried coriander seeds
0.5 tsp. Turmeric powder

Method

Dry roast on a medium heat all the masala mix apart from the turmeric in a pan. Do not burn.

Cool down the spices and add the turmeric powder.

Roast the coconut in a hot pan until slightly browned and add to the masala mix. Grind all to make a powder mix.

Marinate the meat with salt, lemon juice, and 0.25 tsp. of turmeric powder.

Mix and marinate for 15 minutes.

Fry the onions, ginger, and garlic in the oil on a medium heat in a large saucepan.

When the onions are browned, add the chopped tomatoes.

Continue to cook on a low heat until softened.

Add the marinated meat and curry leaves.

Cook for 10 minutes on a medium heat.

Add all the masala and coconut powder mix, salt, and sugar.

Add the water. If you require more Xacuti gravy, you can add more water based on your preference.

Now allow to boil. Turn the heat down to low when boiled.

Cover and cook for at least 30 to 40 minutes.

Chickpea Xacuti

PREPARATION TIME
10 MINS

COOKING TIME
30 MINS

SERVINGS
4-6

Who says vegetarians can't have all the taste? A twist on the famous Goan Xacuti using chickpeas which are affordable and widely available.

Ingredients

2 x 400g Tins of chickpeas
100g Desiccated coconut
2 Large diced onions
2 Medium-sized chopped tomatoes
25g Chopped fresh ginger
10 Cloves chopped garlic
1 tbsp. Tamarind paste
1 vegetable stock cube
0.5 tsp. Salt
1 tsp. Sugar
450ml Water
2 tbsp. Vegetable oil
Approx. 80g Coriander

Masala mix

2 tsp. dried Chillies
1 tsp. Cumin seeds
0.5 tsp. Black peppercorns
0.5 tsp. Cloves
1 inch long Cinnamon stick
0.25 tsp. Cardamom seeds
1 tsp. Dried Coriander seeds
0.5 tsp. Turmeric powder

Method

Roast the coconut in a hot pan until slightly brown. Take off the heat.

Dry roast on a medium heat all the masala mix apart from the turmeric in a pan. Do not burn. Cool down the spices and add the turmeric powder. Grind all to make a masala mix.

Fry the onions, ginger, and garlic in the oil on a medium heat in a large saucepan.

When the onions are soft, add the chopped tomatoes.

Continue to cook on a low heat until softened.

Add the masala mix and cook for 5 minutes.

Add the drained chickpeas.

Cook for 5 minutes on a medium heat.

Add the roasted coconut, salt, sugar, and tamarind. Stir well.

Add the water. (If you require more Xacuti gravy, you can add more water based on your preference)

Allow to cook on a low heat with the lid on for another 15 minutes.

Stir in the coriander leaves and serve.

Spicy Noodles the Goan way

PREPARATION TIME
10 MINS

COOKING TIME
15 MINS

SERVINGS
4

Visit Goa today, and you will see a fusion of Indo-Chino cuisine with noodles and Oriental inspired dishes on the menus.

That's why I love the variety of cuisine and exotic tastes when I am in Goa.

Ingredients

250g Thin pasta noodles (cooked)

350g Fresh king prawns (deveined)

8 Sliced spring onions. (ensure you keep the sliced white bulbs separate from the green tops)

1 Finely chopped garlic bulb

1 Sliced pepper (red, yellow, or orange, it does not matter)

7 tbsp. Passata

8 tbsp. Hot and sweet sauce (I like to use Maggi hot and sweet sauce)

2 tsp. Chilli flakes

0.5 tsp. Salt

0.5 tsp. Pepper

4 tbsp. Vegetable oil (for frying)

Method

Add salt, pepper, and chilli flakes to the prawns.

Mix and leave aside.

Heat the oil on a medium heat in a large frypan or wok. Fry the garlic. Do not burn, otherwise, the garlic will taste bitter.

Add the prawns and fry until they turn pink.

Add the sliced white bulbs of the spring onions and the sliced pepper. Mix well and cook for a minute.

Add the Passata, hot sauce and cook for another minute.

Add the cooked pasta noodles and stir well.

Add the green tops of the spring onions, stir.

Take off the heat and serve.

Tip 😊
You can substitute the prawn with Chicken, Tofu, or a Soya substitute.

Spicy meatballs made Goan

 **PREPARATION TIME** 20 MINS

 COOKING TIME 20 MINS

 **SERVINGS** 4

I sometimes find meatballs quite bland, so here is a curried version that will become a family meal favourite. It's bursting with flavour, and can be eaten with rice, pasta, potatoes, or with a salad. If you are vegetarian, you can use soya mince instead.

Ingredients

500g Lamb or beef mince
4 Finely chopped onions
6 Cloves finely chopped garlic
30g Finely chopped ginger
1 tsp. Salt
0.25 tsp. Turmeric
0.5 tsp. Kashmiri chilli powder
1 tsp. Garam masala

Approx. 30g Chopped coriander leaves
4 tbsp. Vegetable oil
220g Passata
1 tbsp. Sugar
230g Water
Optional: Additional chopped coriander & green chillies

Spice mix

1 tsp. Coriander powder
1 tsp. Cumin powder
0.5 tsp. Cinnamon powder
0.5 tsp. Black pepper
0.5 tsp. Clove powder
0.5 tsp. Cardamom powder
0.5 tsp. Garam masala powder
2 tsp. Kashmiri chilli powder
0.5 tsp. Turmeric powder
2 tbsp. Water

Method

Place the mince in a bowl. Take equal quantities of the chopped onion, garlic, and ginger to make up 2 tbsp of mixture, and add to the mince.

Add 0.5 tsp. salt, 0.25 tsp. turmeric, 0.5 tsp. Kashmiri chilli powder, 1 tsp. Garam masala, and chopped coriander leaves. Mix together well.

Form the mixture into small meatballs and place in the fridge for at least 15 minutes to set.

Heat oil in a deep fry pan or wok. Ensure you have a lid.

Fry the rest of the onions, garlic, and ginger on a medium heat until softened.

Turn down the heat, cover, and allow to cook for another few minutes.

Add the meatballs to the pan and allow to cook for a further 10 minutes.

Tip 😊

For an extra creamy dish, try adding some cream or natural yogurt.

Mix the 2 tbsp. of water to the spice mix to make a masala and add to the pan.

Add the Passata, the sugar, rest of the salt, and the rest of the water. Mix carefully to ensure the meatballs do not break.

Cover the pan and allow to cook on a low heat for at least another 10 minutes.

When ready, sprinkle a handful of chopped coriander on top and serve.

Chicken Tikka masala my way

PREPARATION TIME
4 HOURS 15 MINUTES, INCLUDING THE MARINATING TIME

COOKING TIME
25 MINS

SERVINGS
4-6

This dish is one of my favourites. I like to eat it rolled in a paratha or stuffed into a Goan puri. Nothing stops you from making this a vegetarian tikka dish with meaty vegetables like roasted aubergine or oyster mushrooms.

Ingredients

4 Chicken breasts cut into pieces

Coriander leaves for garnish (optional)

Spice mix

0.25 tsp. Turmeric powder
0.25 tsp. Chilli powder
0.5 tsp. Coriander powder
1 tsp. Cumin powder
0.5 tsp. Garam masala

To make the marinade

Juice of 1 lemon
300g Natural yogurt
10g Chopped garlic & 10g chopped ginger
1 tsp. Kashmiri chilli powder
1 tsp. Garam masala
0.5 tsp. Salt
1 tsp. Vegetable oil

To make the Tikka gravy

1 Medium chopped onion
10g Chopped Garlic & 10g chopped ginger
250g Tomato passata
1 tbsp. Tomato puree
300ml Water
2 tbsp. Vegetable oil (for frying)
6 tsp. Single cream

Method

Make up the marinade with all the ingredients.

Pour over the chicken and allow it to marinate for at least 4 hours in a fridge.

Once the chicken has marinated, place the chicken pieces under a hot grill until slightly charcoaled. It will take approx. 5-10 minutes. Take out and leave aside while you make the Tikka gravy.

Now make the Tikka gravy

Fry the onion, ginger, and garlic in the oil on a medium heat in a deep pan until softened.

Add all the spice mix.

Tip 😊

If you are making this a vegetarian dish, roast the vegetables first, to ensure they stay firm, and to enable better absorption of the spices.

Add the tomato passata, tomato puree and mix well.

Cook on a medium heat for 5 minutes.

Add the grilled chicken.

Add the water and allow it to boil.

Cover and cook for 10-15 minutes on a low heat.

Once cooked, swirl in the cream.

Garnish with coriander when serving.

Sorpotel

PREPARATION TIME
20 MINUTES

COOKING TIME
1 HOUR

SERVINGS
4-6

No Goan dinner party would be complete without the Sorpotel influenced by the Portuguese. Made with vinegar and pork, you will not have tasted a curry like this anywhere else. Again, another party favourite.

Ingredients

1 Kilo belly of skinned pork meat
0.5 tsp. Turmeric powder
2 Star anise
1-inch Cinnamon stick
0.5 tsp. Of salt
600ml (1 pint) Of water

150ml Vinegar
1 tsp. Sugar
1 tsp. Salt
2 tbsp. Paprika
0.5 tsp. Turmeric powder
2 tbsp. Kashmiri chilli powder
250g Passata

Spice mix

1 tsp. Cumin seeds
0.5 inch Cinnamon stick
0.5 tsp. Black peppercorns
0.5 tsp. Cloves
0.5 tsp. Cardamom seeds

Gravy mix

3 Chopped onions
20 Curry leaves

25g Chopped ginger
2 tbsp. Oil

12 Cloves of chopped garlic

Method

Place the pork meat in a large saucepan with a lid. Add the salt, turmeric, star anise, and cinnamon stick.

Add the water and allow it to boil. Then, take off the heat and cool down.

When the meat has cooled, take it out of the water. Remove the star anise and cinnamon.

Do not throw the meat water out. You will need it to make the gravy later.

Cut the meat into small quarter inch cubes.

Heat the oven until it is very hot. Place the meat cubes on a large tray and bake in the oven for 15 minutes. Make sure the meat does not burn.

After 15 minutes, take the meat out and cool down.

Tip 😊

If you are not a red meat eater, you can substitute with chicken which tastes just as good.

I like to eat this with fried potatoes or Sana.

Now prepare the spice mix.

Grind all the spices. You can substitute with ready-made powders, but the taste will not be as authentic.

Add the paprika, chilli powder, turmeric, sugar, salt, and vinegar. Stir well to make a paste.

Now make the gravy mix

Fry the onions, ginger, and garlic in the oil on a medium heat.

When the onions are browned, add the curry leaves.

Add the spice mix paste and cook for a further 10 minutes on a medium heat.

Add the pork meat, the meat water, and the Passata.

Allow to boil, and then turn the heat down to low.

Cover and cook for at least 15 minutes before it is ready to be served.

Goan Fish Curry

PREPARATION TIME
15 MINUTES

COOKING TIME
25 MINUTES

SERVINGS
4

Fish and Shellfish are a standard part of the cuisine in Goa, and there are many variations to the traditional Goan fish curry, but here is mine.

Just select which fish you would like to use. Pomfret, Mackerel, and Kingfish are normally used, but you can also use Salmon or Prawns. I am going to use Salmon here, which is readily available everywhere.

Ingredients

6 Fillets of salmon. Approx. 750g.

0.5 tsp. Kashmiri chilli powder

0.5 tsp. Turmeric powder

2 Finely chopped medium onions

20-25g Finely chopped ginger

30-35g Finely chopped garlic

5 tbsp. Vegetable oil

4 tbsp. Passata

1 x 400ml Can of coconut milk

2 tbsp. Tamarind paste

1 tbsp. Sugar

1 tsp. Salt

50g Chopped coriander

Approx. 150ml of water if you require a thinner curry.

Optional: green or red chillies for heat depending on your preference

Spice paste

2 tsp. Coriander powder

1 tsp. Cumin powder

0.5 tsp. Black pepper

1.5 tsp. Kashmiri Chilli Powder

1 tsp. Turmeric powder

1 tbsp. Water

Method

Skin the salmon fillets. Cut in half. Add 0.5 tsp. Kashmiri chilli powder and 0.5 tsp. turmeric powder and leave aside.

Make the spice paste by mixing the ingredients together with the water.

Fry ginger, onions, and garlic on a medium heat in the oil until browned. Add 1 tsp. salt halfway through the cooking. Turn the heat down.

Add the Passata and the spice paste to the pan and mix well.

Add the coconut milk, sugar, and tamarind to the pan.

Turn up the heat slightly and allow to cook for 5 minutes. Add any chillies now if you require a spicier curry.

Tip 😊

Curries don't have to be eaten with rice. My children like to eat this one with mashed potato. I know it sounds a little strange, but the intensity and creaminess of the curry compliments the potato so well.

Add the salmon pieces. Turn the heat up and allow to boil.

Lower the heat, and cover. Cook for a further 10-15 minutes.

When cooked, sprinkle chopped coriander leaves into the curry. Mix and serve.

Okra and Prawn Curry

PREPARATION TIME
10 MINUTES

COOKING TIME
25 MINUTES

SERVINGS
4

This is an adaptation to the fish curry with an added vegetable, the humble but exotic Okra.

In fact, you can go totally vegan and just leave the prawn out. Just remember to increase the quantity of vegetables or add substitutes like Tofu.

Ingredients

400g Uncooked prawns- deveined

500g Okra vegetable

0.5 tsp. Turmeric

2 Medium-chopped onions

20-25g Chopped ginger

10 Cloves of chopped garlic

3 Medium chopped tomatoes

2 Whole green chillies

400ml can of coconut milk

3 tbsp. Tamarind

1 tsp. Sugar

0.5 tsp. Salt

150ml of Water

3 tbsp. Vegetable oil

Spice Mix

1 tsp. Turmeric

0.5 tsp. Cumin powder

0.5 tsp. Coriander powder

0.5 tsp. Garam masala

0.5 tsp. Chilli powder

0.5 tsp. Paprika powder

Method

Marinate prawns in 0.25 tsp. salt and 0.5 tsp. turmeric and keep aside.

Slice the okra into rounds and discard the stems.

Heat the oil and fry the onions, ginger, and garlic until softened on a medium heat.

Add the okra. Stir and cook for approx. 5 minutes.

Add the chopped tomatoes and cook for a few minutes.

Add the spice mix and cook for a further 5 minutes.

Add the prawns and cook until pink.

Add the coconut milk, tamarind, sugar, the rest of the salt, and green chillies.

Add the water. If you require a thinner curry, add more water.

Allow to boil, and then lower the heat.

Cover and cook for a further 10-15 minutes.

Tip 😊

You can add peppers and roasted aubergine pieces for additional flavour and colour, especially if you are going for the fully vegan option.

Goan Chilli Fry

PREPARATION TIME
10 MINUTES

COOKING TIME
20 MINUTES

SERVINGS
4

This chilli fry has a unique fiery taste down to the vinegar and, dare I say it, a little "ketchup," but it really works. For my vegetarian friends, you can skip the meat and replace it with more meaty vegetables like aubergine and oyster mushrooms instead. This was one of my father's favourites.

Ingredients

2 Chicken breasts (cut into strips)

8 Cloves chopped garlic

15g Chopped ginger

10 Cloves

5g Stick of cinnamon

1 tsp. Salt

1 Large pepper

Approx. 150g mushrooms

3 Sliced onions

1-2 chillies

2 tbsp. Vegetable oil

Masala Mix

50ml Vinegar

6 tbsp. Passata

1 tbsp. Ketchup

1 tsp. Sugar

0.5 tsp. Chilli powder

0.5 tsp. Turmeric powder

1 tsp. Garam masala

Method

Mix all the ingredients of the masala mix together to make a paste.

In a deep fry-pan pan or wok, fry the garlic, ginger, half of the onions, the cloves, and cinnamon in the oil on a medium heat.

Once the onions, garlic, and ginger are slightly browned, add the masala paste. Stir and cook for a minute.

Add the chicken breast strips, stir, and cook for another 10 minutes.

Add the rest of the onions, peppers, mushrooms, and chillies. Continue cooking on a medium heat for another 10 minutes.

Turn off and enjoy.

Tip 😊

Eat on its own or with bread. However, the sweetness and sourness of the dish partners really well with noodles or white rice. You can substitute the chicken with pork strips instead

Stuffed Spice Peppers

PREPARATION TIME
15 MINUTES INCLUDING STAND-TIME

COOKING TIME
25 MINUTES

SERVINGS
4

I really do love my vegetables. They are so versatile and when stuffed can really make a meal on their own. Courgettes, aubergine, marrow, and the humble bell pepper are readily available. This dish is going to use large peppers with a prawn stuffing. Again, you can add a variety of fillings including chicken, mince, soya and rice.

Ingredients

- 350g chopped prawns
- 4 Large Bell Peppers - Use red, yellow or orange for sweetness.
- 3 Medium chopped onions
- 20g Chopped ginger
- 30g Chopped garlic
- 1 tsp. Garam masala
- 0.5 tsp. Cumin powder
- 1 tsp. Turmeric for prawns
- 1 tsp. Chilli Powder
- 3 Green chillies
- 2 Large tomatoes
- 2 Medium potatoes – boiled and mashed
- 3 tbsp. Vegetable oil
- 50g Chopped coriander
- Salt to taste

Method

Mix the prawns with the turmeric and 0.5 tsp. of salt and leave aside.

Fry ginger, garlic, onions and chilli in oil until soft on a medium heat.

Add the tomatoes, garam masala, cumin powder and chilli powder.

Mix and cook until tomatoes are soft.

Add the prawns and cook until pink.

Mix in the mashed potato, and coriander.

Lower the heat, cover and cook for 5-10 minutes.

When cooked, take off the heat and cool down.

Prepare the peppers

Create a cap for the peppers by cutting the top off. Keep the caps aside.

Scoop the insides of the peppers, getting rid of the seeds and any excess white pith.

Tip 😊
You can replace the potato with rice or couscous if you prefer.

Blanch the peppers and the tops for 5 minutes in a big bowl of boiling water.

Take out, get rid of any excess water, and pat dry.

Fill each pepper with the prawn filling, and cover with the top.

Oil the outside of the peppers. Place on an oiled baking tray.

Bake in a medium hot oven for about 15 minutes.

Take out, scoop out, cut open and enjoy any way you want.

Chilli-Cheese Omelette

PREPARATION TIME
5 MINUTES

COOKING TIME
5 MINUTES

SERVINGS
1

When I am on holiday, I always tend to go for an Omelette for breakfast. It makes me feel like I am having a healthy option when there is so much tempting bread and pastries on offer. By now, you will know I don't go for the bland, and that also goes for my omelettes. My mother makes the tastiest omelettes ever, and my childhood friends used to love them.

Omelettes can be so bland otherwise.

Ingredients

2 large eggs

1 tbsp. Ghee, butter or margarine

1 large chilli (depending on heat preference)

Small handful of chopped coriander leaves

1 small chopped tomato

1 small chopped onion

50g Cheese (add more according to preference)

1 sliced small Goan choris sausage. If you can't get this, feel free to add a few chopped pieces of Chorizo instead.

Pinch of salt for taste

Method

Mix all ingredients together.

Melt the Ghee, butter or margarine in a fry pan.

On a medium heat, add the omelette mix to the pan, and allow one side to cook for a few minutes.

Carefully flip to the other side or fold over and cook through.

Tip 😊

This is perfect with my Goan chutney.

You can add a little water to the chutney to make it more of a sauce to eat with the omelette.

Green Goan Garlic Chicken

PREPARATION TIME
1.5 HOURS INCLUDING MARINATE TIME

COOKING TIME
45 MINUTES

SERVINGS
6

This recipe is one originally created by my mother and father. It was an experiment. My father would be by her side as the chief food taster of course, in case it needed a little more of this and that. If you like garlic, like I do, then this one is for you. Cooking the garlic cloves whole brings out the sweetness in them.

Ingredients

1 kilo Skinned Chicken thighs

Juice of 2 medium lemons

Approx. 250g garlic cloves (3 bulbs)

3 tbsp. Vegetable oil

0.5 tsp. Turmeric

0.5 tsp. Cumin powder

1 tsp. Garam masala

2 tsp. Salt

To make the marinade paste

Approx. 100g Coriander

Approx. 10 Medium Green Chillies (Mild)

20g Ginger

10g chopped garlic

2 Medium onions – chopped into large pieces.

250g Plain Greek yoghurt

Method

Cut each chicken thigh in half to help it cook easier.

Add the lemon juice and 1 tsp. salt to the chicken. Mix well and leave aside whilst you make the marinade paste.

Fry the chopped onion with a drop of vegetable oil until slightly charred.

Blend the onion, coriander, ginger, yoghurt, 5 green chillies, and 0.5. tsp salt until it becomes a paste.

Pour over the chicken and leave to marinate between 1-2 hrs.

Heat the vegetable oil in a large pan. A large wok with a lid is perfect.

Add the cloves of garlic and cook for approx. 2 minutes until slightly browned.

Tip 😊

This is quite a dry chicken dish, which makes it perfect for a Chicken and fried potatoes meal.

Add the remaining green chillies.

Add turmeric, cumin powder and 0.5 tsp. salt.

Mix well together.

Add the marinated chicken pieces to the pan, and fry on a medium heat for about 10 minutes.

Add any surplus marinade from the chicken to the pan.

Continue to cook for about 5 minutes.

Now add the garam masala. Stir through. Cover and cook on a low heat for about 30 minutes.

Notes

Use this page to add any adjustments you may want to make to the recipes based on your personal preference and tastes.

Notes

Church Life

Goans take their religion very seriously. Having been ruled under the Portuguese for hundreds of years, the catholic influence is visible everywhere. It extends from gleaming churches to hilltop chapels and roadside altars.

Today, Catholicism blends and merges with other Indian religions seamlessly and peacefully.

You'll find churches in every town and village, with differing architecture and styles.

Masses will be available in Konkani and English if you want to experience this.

Just double-check first.

If you are in the capital Panaji, make sure you climb the steps to the gleaming white" Our lady of the Immaculate Conception" church.

Don't forget to take a trip to Olde Goa, where the most famous and impressive church "The Basilica of Bom Jesus" stands.

The body of Saint Francis Xavier, who died in 1552, still lies there.

His casket is brought down for public viewing every ten years as the body of the saint was not decaying at the rate it should have been. Many claim this to be a miracle, and he is revered in Goa.

Sweet Stuff

Teatime is a big deal for Goans.

A cup of Rose masala tea with a sweet treat is standard!

Goans use coconut, jaggery, semolina, and cardamom in their desserts, making them so distinct.

Bolinha Semolina cookies

PREPARATION TIME
3HRS 10 MINUTES, INCLUDING DOUGH RISE TIME.

COOKING TIME
30 MINUTES

SERVINGS
12-15 COOKIES

Bolinha is a small sweet cookie traditionally served at teatime in Goa. They are made with semolina and coconut. You can buy them everywhere in Goa. They are sweet and crumbly and very moreish! I would compare them to the macaron biscuit.

Ingredients

6 Egg yolks

250g Semolina

300g Sugar

100g Desiccated coconut (or fresh grated coconut if you can get it)

250g Butter

1 tsp. Cardamom powder

1 tsp. Baking powder

Method

Mix all the ingredients together in a bowl until it becomes a soft dough.

Cover the bowl, and keep it aside for at least 3 hours, but do not place it in the fridge.

After 3 hours, take the dough out, divide it into small equally sized round balls, and press slightly down into a fat biscuit shape.

If you want to do it the Goan way, cut a cross shape on the top of each biscuit.

Turn the oven on at a low heat and allow it to warm up.

Place the dough cookies on a greased baking tray.

Bake in the oven at a low heat for 15 minutes.

After 15 minutes, turn the oven on at a high heat and bake for a further 10 minutes until golden.

Take out of the oven and leave to cool.

Tip 😊

If you want to be very naughty, drizzle some melted chocolate over the top of each Bolinha cookie before eating.

Goan Nevri Pastries

PREPARATION TIME
30 MINUTES

COOKING TIME
15 MINUTES

SERVINGS
15-20 NEVRI

These are sweet and simple coconut and semolina pastries. They are a definite Christmas treat in Goa, but they can be enjoyed anytime. If you go to Goa, you can buy specific Nevri pastry cutters which fold over.

Ingredients

For the pastry

400g Plain flour

2 tbsp. Ghee or butter

150ml Water

Vegetable oil for deep frying the Nevri

For the stuffing

250g Semolina

50g Desiccated coconut

300g Sugar

200g Ghee or melted butter

150ml Milk

A handful of chopped mixed nuts

1 tsp. Cardamom powder

0.5 tsp. Salt

Method

Dry roast the semolina in a pan on a medium heat. Please do not allow it to burn.

Dry roast the nuts in a separate pan on a medium heat. Please do not allow it to burn.

Add the melted ghee or butter to the semolina and cook for a minute. Now add the milk and cook for a further minute. Finally, add cardamom, salt, and the roasted nuts. Stir well.

Add the coconut and cook for a few minutes. Leave aside to cool while preparing the pastry.

To make the pastry, mix the flour, Ghee or butter, and water until it becomes a dough. Leave aside for 15 minutes.

Roll the dough out on a floured surface to form a thin layer.

Cut out into 4-inch diameter circular shapes which will then fold over to form a semi-circle pastry.

Place the stuffing into one half of the circle, and fold over to seal in a semi-circle.

You can also make a fluted pattern on the edges with a fork or with your fingers to make them look more attractive.

Heat the oil on a medium heat in a pan. Ensure you have enough oil to cover the Nevri while frying.

Fry the Nevri, and when they are golden, take them out and drain them on a kitchen towel.

Kormolas Anytime Crunch (crunchy pastry twists)

PREPARATION TIME
10 MINUTES

COOKING TIME
10 MINUTES

SERVINGS
IS BASED ON WHETHER YOU WANT TO SHARE THESE OR NOT!

These are going to be the easiest sweet snack you are ever going to make. I always recall that these were the quick bites my mother and I would make every Christmas as a young girl. They were so easy to make. We could spend time together and chat in the kitchen while rolling and frying these sweet and so simple pastries.

Ingredients

200g Plain flour

3 tbsp. Sugar

1 tbsp. Butter, Ghee or oil.

1 tsp. Vanilla essence

60g Semolina

0.5 tsp. Cardamom powder

1 tsp. Baking powder

0.25 tsp. Salt

70ml Warm water

Vegetable oil for deep frying

Icing sugar for dusting the cooked Kormolas

Method

Mix all the ingredients together apart from the oil until you make a biscuit dough. It should be firm.

Roll the dough out on a floured surface to form a thin layer. The thinner the crispier.

Cut the dough into small squares or circles.

Twist with your fingers into shapes

Heat the oil in a deep pan until hot.

Drop the pastry shapes into the oil and fry until golden.

Take out and drain on a paper towel.

Dust with icing sugar.

These can be kept in an airtight container and can be taken out when you have the need or a nibble.

Just beware - they are so moreish you may lose count of how many you have actually eaten which is why I could not provide a serving size!

Bebinca (Rainbow effect optional)

PREPARATION TIME
30 MINUTES

COOKING TIME
60 MINUTES

SERVINGS
8-10

This is the most famous Goan dessert which you can buy pre-packaged when in Goa. However, these don't actually do any justice to the rich taste and I tend to avoid the pre-packaged ones. This dessert is actually a stack of baked pancakes. It takes time and effort, but it's worth the wait but beware, it is not great for your waistline! When baked, it becomes very fudgy in taste and texture.

Ingredients

100g Creamed coconut

Boiling water to soften the creamed coconut

15 Medium egg yolks

300g Sugar

300ml Evaporated milk

0.25 tsp. Nutmeg

1 tsp. Vanilla extract

8 tbsp. Plain flour

0.5 tsp. Salt

250g Ghee or butter to spoon on top of each pancake layer. You may need more or less.

Method

Soften the creamed coconut in its packaging in boiling water.

Place the egg yolks in a large mixing bowl. Add the sugar and beat until light and fluffy.

Add the softened creamed coconut, the evaporated milk, nutmeg, vanilla, and salt.

Add the flour and continue mixing to form a smooth pancake batter. Stand for 15 minutes.

Grease and line a large cake tin.

To achieve the layered rainbow look, separate the batter into equal quantities, and add your choice of food colouring to each.

Heat your grill and ensure it is hot.

Pour enough batter into the cake tin to form the first layer of pancake.

Put under the grill until cooked.

Take out and spoon 0.5 tsp. of the melted ghee or butter on the layer. Add another layer of batter and grill.

Repeat the process of adding equal quantities of batter and ghee or butter for each layer until all the batter is used up.

Tip 😊

This dessert can be served hot or cold and is delicious with ice cream or fresh cream.

For the rainbow effect, alternate the coloured pancake batter when grilling.

Cover the cake tin with foil and bake in a medium-hot oven for 30-40 minutes. To ensure it is cooked through, try piercing a cocktail stick into the batter to see if it has set. It should come out clean.

Once cooked, take it out, and leave it to cool. Then, turn it out of the tin and serve.

A bowl of Vermicelli angel hair dessert

 **PREPARATION TIME** 5 MINUTES

 **COOKING TIME** 10 MINUTES

 **SERVINGS** 4

I believe this dessert was originally made by the Portuguese using egg strands and has a very interesting history if you want to look it up.

It was originally called Angel hair because of the yellow colour and texture.

My easy option is to use thin strands of Vermicelli for a quick dessert which is a lot simpler to make.

Ingredients

150g Vermicelli

80g melted salted butter

80g sugar

0.5 tsp. Saffron essence (optional)

0.5 tsp. Cardamom powder

0.5 tsp. Vanilla essence

Approx. 350ml of milk

Handful Roasted coconut flakes

Handful of Roasted chopped nuts (Optional)

Method

Dry roast the Vermicelli in a pan on a low heat for a few minutes. Do not burn.

Take off the heat, and add the melted butter, and mix well.

Add the cardamom, sugar and saffron essence.

Add the milk, stir well, and put back on heat and allow to boil, mixing throughout.

Once boiled, take off the heat, and add the coconut flakes on top.

For extra nuttiness and taste, add chopped roasted nuts.

Coconut & Jaggery Pancakes

PREPARATION TIME
10 MINUTES

COOKING TIME
15 MINUTES

SERVINGS
8 PANCAKES

The humble pancake has been transformed into a sweet coconut dessert. The difference is in the filling, which is a truly Goan addition.

Ingredients

To make the Pancake mix

2 Eggs

240g Plain flour

0.5 tsp. Salt

40g Melted butter

350ml Milk

Pancake filling

100g Jaggery sugar chunks

100ml Coconut water (to melt the jaggery)

Approx. 80g Desiccated coconut

Optional: Chopped nuts

Enough butter to fry the pancakes in a fry pan

Method

Place all the pancake mix ingredients in a bowl.

Mix well to create a smooth batter. I like to use a hand blender to get the lumps out. Leave aside while you make the filling.

Melt the jaggery chunks with the coconut milk in a pan on a medium to low heat.

Once melted, mix in the desiccated coconut and turn the heat off.

Optional: You can also add chopped nuts to the filling at this stage.

Heat a tsp. of butter in a hot fry pan. Place a ladle of pancake mixture in the pan. Swirl around the pan to ensure an even pancake. Fry on both sides until golden.

Flip out of the pan on a plate and add a generous amount of the filling in the middle of the pancake.

Roll, eat and repeat!

Notes

Use this page to add any adjustments you may want to make to the recipes based on your personal preference and tastes.

On the spice trail

Whenever I am in Goa, I always make time to visit a spice garden. You'll find a number of spice gardens dotted around, and they are easily signposted if you want to jump on a motorbike and visit at your leisure. That's my preference anyway!

And it won't just be spices you'll be introduced to like cinnamon, cloves or turmeric.

These gardens will also show you the wonders of naturally grown fruits, seeds, nuts, coffee-beans and even cacao pods.

Most will also be able to show you the fermentation process of the Feni alcohol.

Your guide will make it a fun, interactive, and informative experience.

I remember the first time I visited, my children who were very young then and myself were amazed that pineapples actually grow on the ground and not high up on a tree.

It's a great educational taste, touch and smell experience for the whole family.

Most spice gardens will also include a traditional Indian buffet meal at the end of your spice journey and a glass of the Coconut Feni to down in one.

You'll be able to purchase spices, natural oils, and all sorts of herbal powders at the Spice gardens at affordable prices.

I would always recommend a morning visit, as it can get busy in the high season with tourists. I always like to go earlier in the morning when it's generally quieter as I tend to get a spice guide all to myself.

A bit about Goan Pickles

A dish would not be complete without traditional Goan pickles.

By now, you know Goans love their seafood, so nothing can be better than the famous **Prawn Balchao pickle**. Balchao is a well-known spicy prawn masala pickle that can also be eaten as a Goan seafood tapas.

I like taking a jar of this pickle with a fresh baguette and a bottle of wine for picnic time.

Eat it with rice or pasta or do it the Goa way and spread it on hot toast.

The Goan Tendli pickle is made with the crisp ivy gourd vegetable in a spicy and sweet masala. The vegetable is dried out so that it is crunchy and crisp. It is perfect with a Poppadum and as an accompaniment to a traditional meal.

Please note that this pickle generally includes mustard in the ground and seed form in the ingredients.

The Recheado Masala is the traditional Goan masala used everywhere in Goa.

This masala is used as an everyday staple to stuff fish like mackerel before going into the fry pan.
I however like to throw my stuffed Recheado fish and prawns on a barbecue.

You can also use it to stuff vegetables or as a stir fry base to give a spicy kick.

It is vinegar and oil-based and will last in your fridge for months.

Come on, I know you want to spice up your food the Goan way.

So, we have come to the end of the Goan journey. It was a joy to share my favourite recipes, cultural insights and personal memories with you. There are many more recipes I have in my kitchen, but I am keeping them to share with you at another time.

I dedicate the book to my mother, the best cook in the world who has taught me so much, and to my father who was the best Chief food taster in the world.

With love

Katie

www.ingramcontent.com/pod-product-compliance
Lightning Source LLC
Chambersburg PA
CBHW041220240426
43661CB00012B/1093